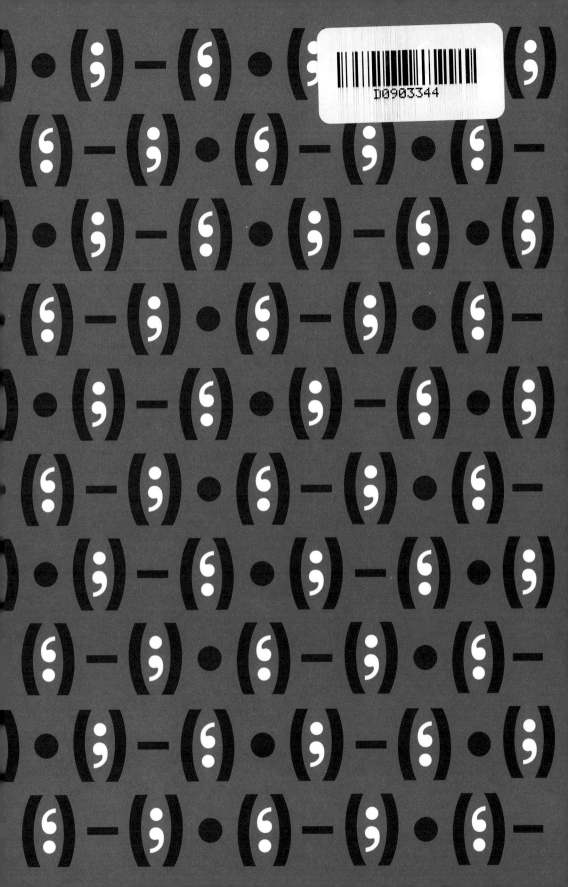

CHRISTIAN MORGENSTERN

IN THE LAND OF
/'PUN(C)TU-'A'{T}IO;N

Illustrated by Rathna Ramanathan

Translated from the German by Sirish Rao

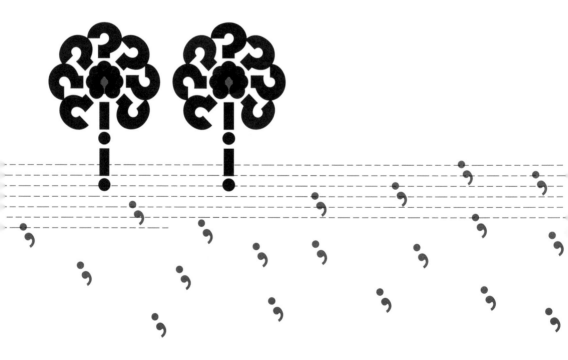

The peaceful land of Punctuation
is filled with tension overnight

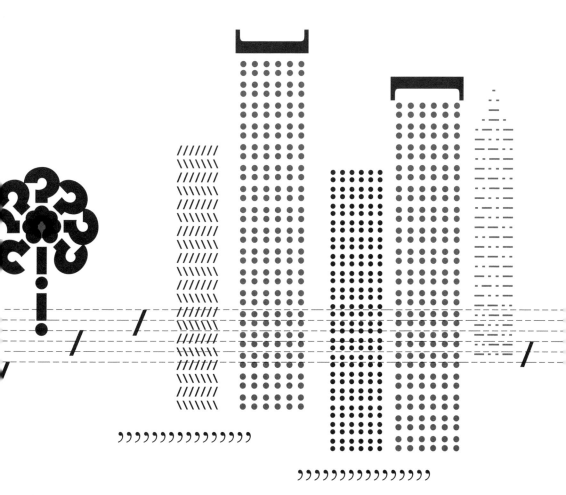

When the stops and commas of the nation
call the semicolons 'parasites'

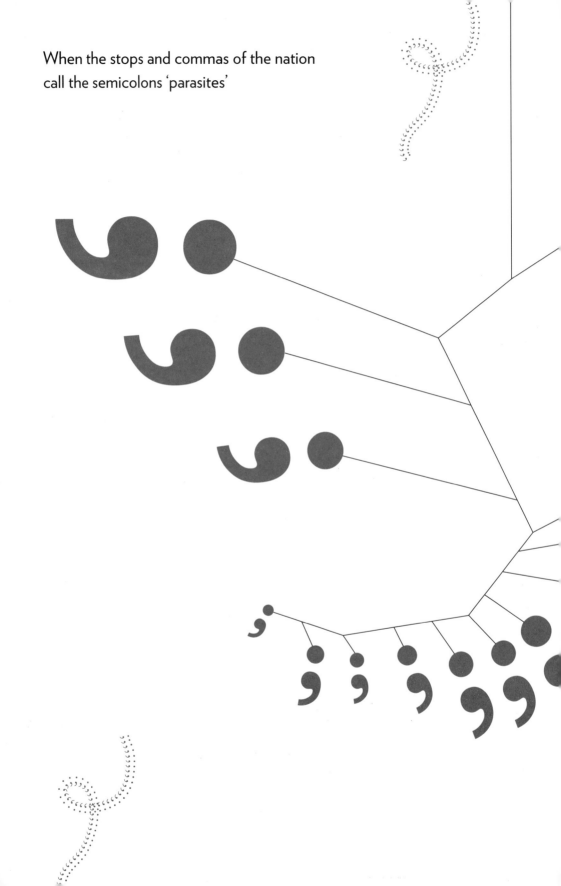

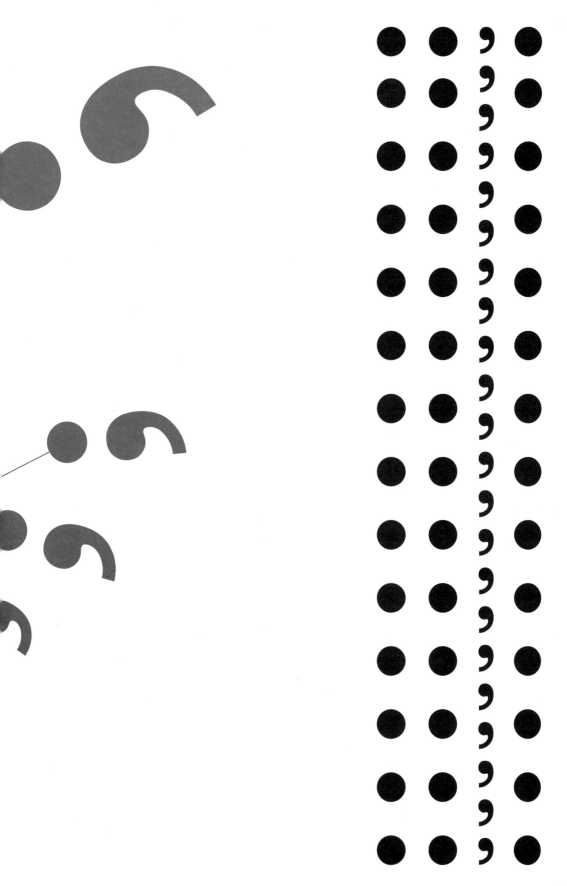

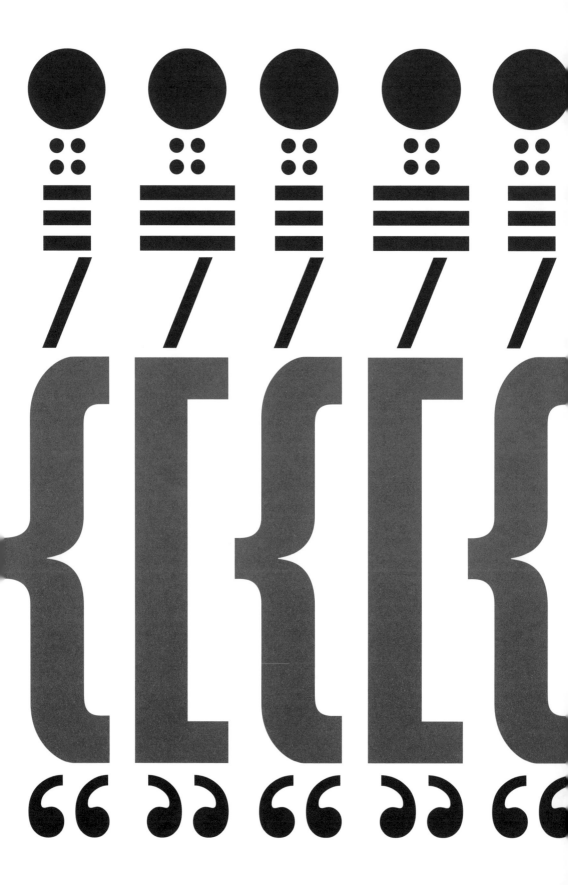

Within the hour they form their troops,
an anti-semicolon group

The question marks avoid the scrape
(as always) and quietly escape

The semicolons' mournful racket
is drowned out by surrounding brackets

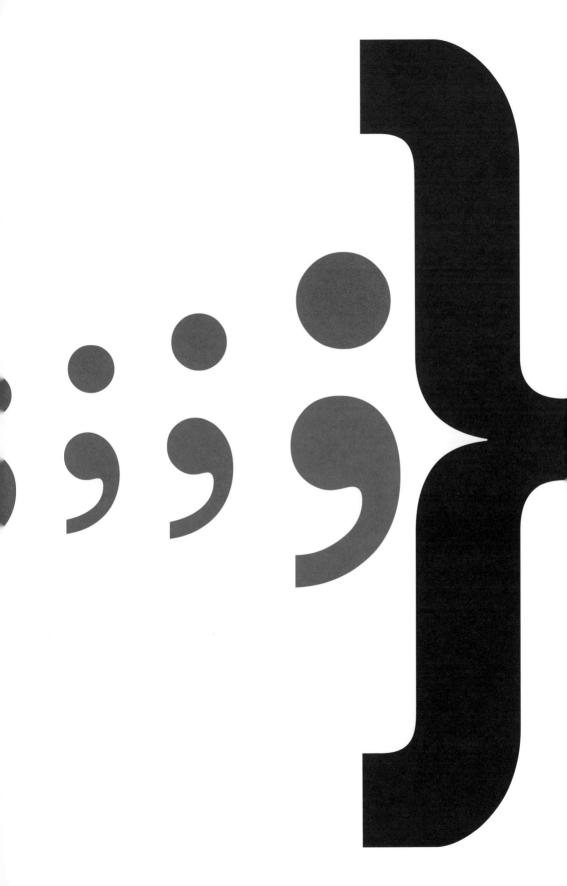

And then the captured creatures freeze
Imprisoned by parentheses

The dreaded minus sign arrives
and - slash! - ends the captives' lives

The question marks, now homeward-bound,
pity the corpses on the ground

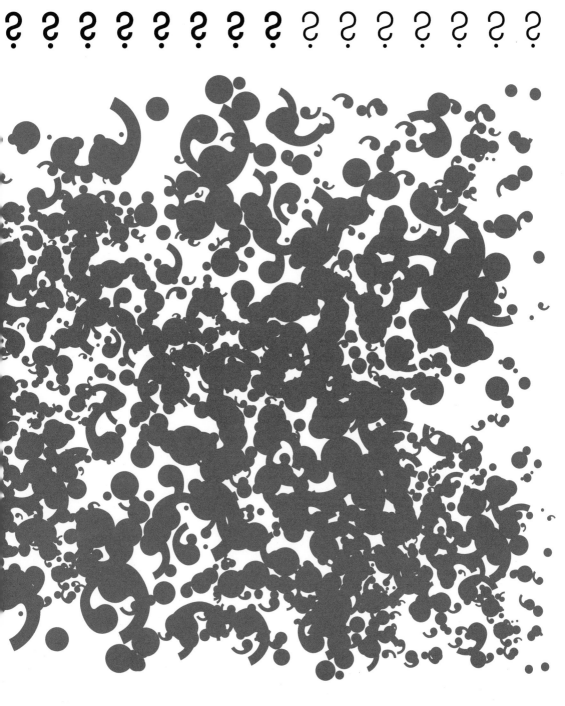

But, woe! A new war looms large,
as dashes against commas charge

And cut across the commas necks
so that the beheaded wrecks

(the dashes delight in gore)
as semi-colons hit the floor.

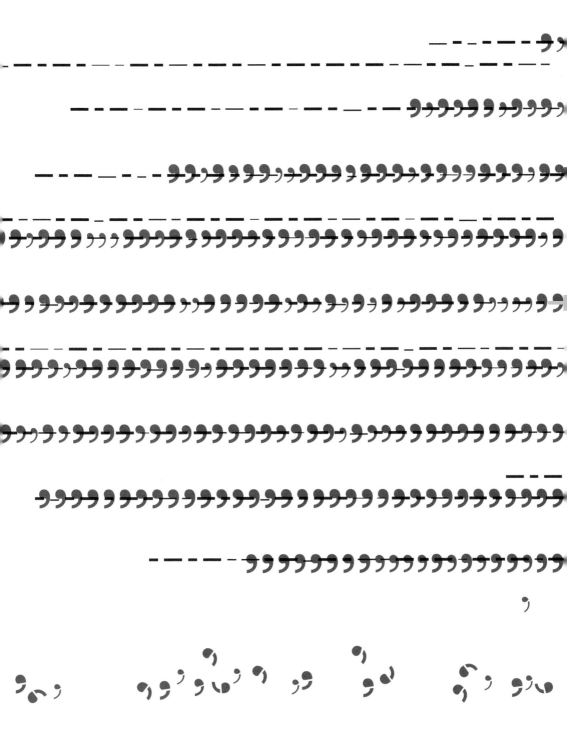

Both semicolon types they bury
in silence in the cemetery

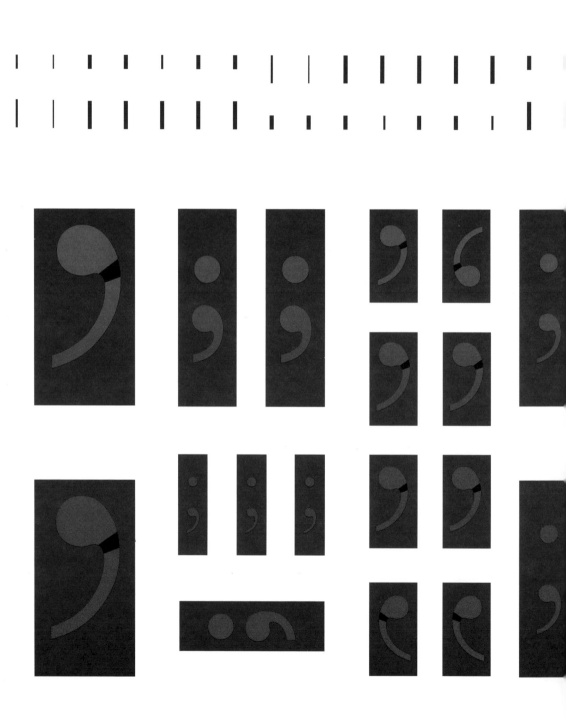

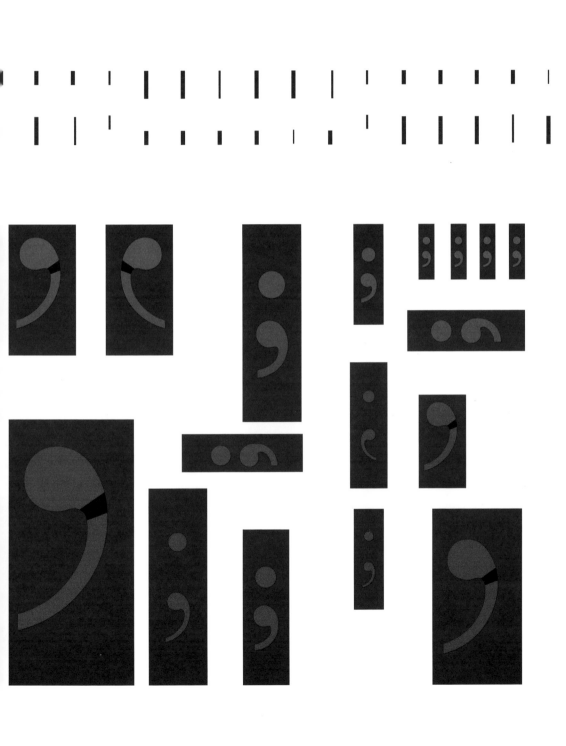

Those dashes that still remain,
Creep blackly behind the mourning train

The exclamation holds a sermon
with colon's help, right on the spot

Then through their comma-form free nation
They all march home: dash dot dash dot

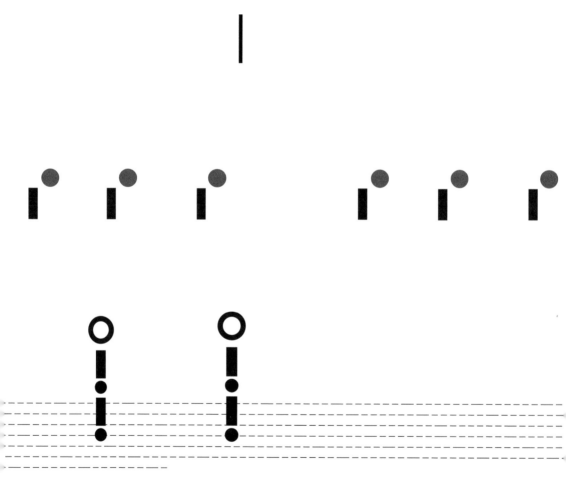

IM REICH DER INTERPUNKTIONEN

Im Reich der Interpunktionen
night fürder goldner Friede prunkt:

Die Semikolons werden Drohnen
genannt von Beistrich und von Punkt.

Es bildet sich zur selben Stund
ein Antisemikolonbund.

Die einzigen, die stumm entweichen
(wie immer), sind die Fragezeichen.

Die Semikolons, die sehr jammern,
umstellt man mit geschwungen Klammern

und setzt so gefangnen Wesen
noch obendrein in Parenthesen.

Das Minuszeichen naht und-schwapp!
Da zieht es sie vom Leben ab.

Kopfschüttelnd blicken auf die Leichen
die heimgekehrten Fragezeichen.

Doch, Wehe! neuer Kampf sich schürzt:
Gedankenstrich auf Komma stürztund

fährt ihm schneidend durch den Halsbis
dieser gleich-und ebenfalls

(wie jener mörderisch bezweckt)
als Strichpunkt das Gefild bedeckt! ...

Stumm trägt man auf den Totengarten
die Semikolons beider Arten.

Was übrig von Gedankenstreichen,
kommt schwarz und schweigsam nachgeschlichen.

Das Ausrufzeichen hält die Predigt;
das Kolon dient ihm als Adjunkt.

Dann, jeder Kommaform entledigt,
stapft heimwärts, Strich, Punkt, Strich, Punkt . . .

IN THE LAND OF PUNCTUATION

The peaceful land of Punctuation
is filled with tension overnight

When the stops and commas of the nation
call the semicolons 'parasites.'

Within the hour they form their troops,
an anti-semicolon group.

The question marks avoid the scrape
(as always) and quietly escape.

The semicolons' mournful racket
is drowned out by surrounding brackets.

And then the captured creatures freeze,
imprisoned by parentheses.

The dreaded minus sign arrives
and-slash!-ends the captives' lives

The question marks, now homeward-bound,
pity the corpses on the ground.

But, woe! A new war looms large,
as dashes against commas charge

and cut across the commas necks
so that the beheaded wrecks

(the dashes delight in gore)
as semi-colons hit the floor.

Both semicolon types they bury
In silence in the cemetery.

Those dashes that still remain
Creep blackly behind the mourning train.

The exclamation holds a sermon
with colon's help, right on the spot

Then through their comma-form free nation
They all march home: dash dot dash dot

IN THE LAND OF PUNCTUATION

Copyright © 2009 Tara Books

For the translation: Sirish Rao
For the illustration: Rathna Ramanathan

For this edition:
Tara Books, www.tarabooks.com
Design: Rathna Ramanathan   www.m9design.com
Production: C Arumugam
Printed in China by Leo Paper Products Limited

ISBN: 978-81-907546-0-6